RAND | PROJECT AIR FORCE

The Creation of the PLA Strategic Support Force and Its Implications for Chinese Military Space Operations

Kevin L. Pollpeter, Michael S. Chase, Eric Heginbotham

Prepared for the United States Air Force

Approved for public release; distribution unlimited

For more information on this publication, visit www.rand.org/t/RR2058

Library of Congress Cataloging-in-Publication Data is available for this publication.
ISBN: 978-0-8330-9872-6

Published by the RAND Corporation, Santa Monica, Calif.
© Copyright 2017 RAND Corporation
RAND® is a registered trademark.

Support RAND
Make a tax-deductible charitable contribution at
www.rand.org/giving/contribute

www.rand.org

Preface

This report is based on RAND Project AIR FORCE Strategy and Doctrine Program research that was presented at the second China Aerospace Studies Institute conference, sponsored by Headquarters, U.S. Air Force. It was held at RAND's Arlington, Va., office and took place on May 2, 2016. Experts on airpower, military operations, and Chinese military modernization participated in the conference and provided valuable feedback to the report authors. The resulting reports assess notable developments and implications of China's emerging aerospace expeditionary and power projection capabilities.

As China's economic, diplomatic, and security interests continue to expand, the People's Liberation Army (PLA) and, in particular, its aerospace forces—including Air Force, Naval Aviation, and space capabilities—will require more robust power projection and expeditionary capabilities on a par with China's expanding global footprint. In addition to traditional security concerns like Taiwan and maritime territorial disputes, such issues as countering terrorism, humanitarian assistance/disaster relief, and sea-lane protection have now become factors in the PLA's training, doctrine, and modernization efforts. In addition, command of space, including the military use of outer space, is of increasing interest to the PLA as it seeks to develop new capabilities and operating concepts to support its growing range of military missions. This report focuses on the establishment of the PLA's Strategic Support Force (SSF), which was announced on December 31, 2015. The SSF is charged with overseeing Chinese military space, cyber, and electronic warfare capabilities, and its development will have important implications for China's emerging aerospace expeditionary and power projection capabilities.

RAND Project AIR FORCE

RAND Project AIR FORCE (PAF), a division of the RAND Corporation, is the U.S. Air Force's federally funded research and development center for studies and analyses. PAF provides the Air Force with independent analyses of policy alternatives affecting the development, employment, combat readiness, and support of current and future air, space, and cyber forces. Research is conducted in four programs: Force Modernization and Employment; Manpower, Personnel, and Training; Resource Management; and Strategy and Doctrine. The research reported here was prepared under contract FA7014-16-D-1000.

Additional information about PAF is available on our website: www.rand.org/paf

This report documents work originally shared with the U.S. Air Force in May 2016. The draft report, issued on March 1, 2017, was reviewed by formal peer reviewers and U.S. Air Force subject-matter experts.

Contents

Tables

Summary

This report explores the missions and organization of China's military space enterprise. It focuses on the organizational structure of the People's Liberation Army (PLA) Strategic Support Force (SSF). Created on December 31, 2015, as part of a major reorganization of China's military, the SSF is charged with developing and employing most of the PLA's space capabilities. Tasked with integrating space more closely into operations, the creation of the SSF signifies an important shift in the PLA's prioritization of space and portends an increased role for PLA space capabilities. Indeed, Chinese military strategists see military space capabilities and operations as vital in at least three different ways. First, they are a key component of strategic deterrence. Second, they are critical to enabling the PLA to fight informatized local wars and counter U.S. military intervention in the region. Third, they are essential when it comes to supporting operations aimed at protecting China's emerging interests in more-distant parts of the world.

Although little official information exists on the SSF, it does not appear to be a service, nor does it appear to be equivalent to a PLA theater command or a U.S.-style unified command. The SSF appears to be composed of former General Staff Department (GSD) and General Armament Department (GAD) units. Sources indicate that it is composed of a Space Systems Department responsible for the launch and operation of satellites and a Network Systems Department responsible for cyber and electronic warfare (EW).

The main function of the SSF's space component appears to be the launch and operation of satellites to provide the PLA with command and control, communications, computers, intelligence, surveillance, and reconnaissance (C4ISR) capabilities. This includes space-based reconnaissance, communications, and navigation capabilities. Less certain, however, is the scope of the force's counterspace mission. Based on its launch and satellite-operations functions, the SSF's Space Systems Department appears to be responsible at least for the co-orbital counterspace mission. The SSF's Network Systems unit also suggests that the force is responsible for jamming satellite communications and Global Positioning System (GPS) signals, as well as computer network operations against space facilities and satellites. Other counterspace capabilities, like direct-ascent capabilities, may have been retained by other parts of the PLA, although it is also possible that such capabilities have been transferred to the SSF without public announcement. All of these functions also give the SSF an important role in China's approach to strategic deterrence, which encompasses nuclear, conventional, space and counterspace, and cyber warfare capabilities.

The relationship of the SSF to other components of the PLA remains somewhat unclear. For example, China has not publicly announced which unit the SSF reports to or how the SSF coordinates with the services. One possibility is that the SSF reports to the Central Military

Commission (CMC) Joint Staff Department during peacetime, while its units would be attached to a theater command during wartime. It is also as yet unclear how the SSF coordinates with the other military organizations and civilian agencies that perform space missions. This suggests that some sort of joint organization focused on space would have to be set up under a theater command to coordinate and lead the space forces involved in a military operation.

The designation of the SSF to carry out major portions of the space mission indicates that space will be further integrated into PLA warfighting through the development of capabilities, doctrine, and personnel. The establishment of an organization charged with the information-warfare mission suggests that principles need to be established to guide its peacetime development and wartime use. It also suggests that the PLA will need to develop avenues for the promotion of information warfighters and their integration into theater command operations. By integrating space, cyber, and EW, the establishment of the SSF gives China a military space and information-warfare organization that is different from those that handle these missions for the United States and its allies. Although many questions remain unanswered, the creation of the SSF suggests that information warfare, including space warfare, long identified by PLA analysts as a critical element of future military operations, appears to have entered a new phase of development in the PLA, one in which an emphasis on space and information warfare, long-range precision strikes, and the requirements associated with conducting operations at greater distances from China has necessitated the establishment of a new and different type of organization.

Acknowledgments

The authors would like to thank Cortez Cooper, Maj Christopher Stone, and Chris Twomey for their constructive comments and detailed feedback on earlier drafts of this report.

Abbreviations

AMS	Academy of Military Science
ASAT	anti-satellite
C4ISR	command and control, communications, computers, intelligence, surveillance, and reconnaissance
CAS	Chinese Academy of Sciences
CCP	National Congress of the Communist Party of China
CMC	Central Military Commission
CMSA	China Manned Space Agency
EDD	Equipment Development Department
EW	electronic warfare
GAD	General Armament Department
GLD	General Logistics Department
GPD	General Political Department
GPS	Global Positioning System
GSD	General Staff Department
ISR	intelligence, surveillance, and reconnaissance
LTG	Lieutenant General
MR	military region
NASA	National Aeronautics and Space Administration
PAF	Project AIR FORCE
PC	political commissar
PLA	People's Liberation Army
PLAAF	People's Liberation Army Air Force
R&D	research and development
SASTIND	State Administration for Science, Technology and Industry for National Defense
SOSO	system-of-systems operations
SSF	Strategic Support Force
TT&C	telemetry, tracking, and control
USAF	United States Air Force

1. Introduction

Outer space is playing an increasingly important role in the People's Liberation Army's (PLA's) thinking about future military operations. PLA strategists emphasize the crucial role of space in the struggle to gain and maintain information dominance, which they see as deciding the outcome of future military operations. Indeed, as the PLA develops long-range weapon systems capable of striking U.S. military bases and naval vessels, the PLA requires an increasingly sophisticated command and control, communications, computers, intelligence, surveillance, and reconnaissance (C4ISR) system, including the use of a space-based C4ISR architecture, to locate and track these targets. Recognizing the importance of space to military operations, the PLA is also developing a wide range of counterspace systems to deny adversaries the use of space. These changes are represented in China's May 2015 defense white paper, which for the first time officially designated space as a military domain. This was followed by the creation of the PLA Strategic Support Force (SSF) on December 31, 2015. The establishment of the SSF to take over much of China's military space mission is part of a sweeping reorganization of the PLA that reflects this growing emphasis on space and, more broadly, on information warfare. Tasked with integrating space more closely into operations, the SSF signifies an important shift in the PLA's prioritization of space and portends an increased role for space capabilities in Chinese military operations.

This report explores the missions and organization of China's military space enterprise by examining the organizational structure of the newly created SSF. Although numerous news articles have been published about the SSF, little official explanation of its composition and role has been released. In an attempt to add greater clarity to our knowledge of the SSF and, in turn, China's military space program, this report examines what we know about the SSF and then offers informed analysis on its organization and role, especially in regard to the PLA's use of space. We assess that the SSF has been charged with developing and employing space, cyber, and electronic warfare (EW) capabilities and that, in doing so, it has absorbed space-related organizations from the former General Staff Department (GSD) and General Armament Department (GAD), which were eliminated as part of the wide-ranging PLA reorganization. We believe that the creation of the SSF was not intended to streamline all of China's space enterprise under one command, but was instead intended to facilitate joint operations by providing operational commands with the information-warfare infrastructure necessary to conduct "informatized local wars." This appears to include missions formerly assigned to the GSD and GAD, such as the launch and operation of China's space-based C4ISR architecture, but it probably does not include all space and counterspace missions. Some of these could still belong to the other parts of the PLA. In some cases, however, the intended role of the SSF is unclear, because China has not publicly released detailed information. For example, on one hand, it could make sense for the direct-ascent anti-satellite (ASAT) mission to be the responsibility of the PLA Rocket Force, given its experience with the operation of mobile missiles. On the other hand, it could make sense for the mission to be transferred to the SSF so that it would have more unified control over counterspace capabilities that could play important roles in strategic deterrence or joint combat operations.

Furthermore, the SSF may not have been created to be an executive agent for all of China's space enterprise, a reform called for by some in the space program, nor is it necessarily a venue for one service to command China's entire space force, as some military analysts have proposed. Yet the creation of the SSF has moved the sizable portion of China's space program that was formerly under the research and development (R&D)–oriented GAD to the more operationally focused SSF, and the significance of the SSF's establishment should not be underestimated. Its creation heralds a more prominent role for space in PLA operations and suggests the continued building of a more robust space program to meet operational requirements. The establishment of the SSF also suggests that the organization's requirement to train the next generation of space warfighters will necessitate the development of a formal doctrine governing space operations. Ultimately, the creation of the SSF, the establishment of doctrine, and the continued development of space technologies may result in the designation of the SSF as a service responsible for an independent information-warfare campaign, which would include space, cyber, and EW forces.

2. Why Space Is Important to the PLA

The creation of the SSF comes at a time when outer space is playing an increasingly important role in the PLA's concept of warfighting. Although PLA analysts have for years written on the importance of space to military operations,[1] the official designation of space as a new domain did not occur until the 2015 defense white paper.[2] This elevation of space is an outcome of a series of major military reforms called for by the Third Plenum of the 18th Party Congress, intended to enable the PLA to better conduct joint operations and utilize advanced technologies.

Among the most important of these reforms was the call to adjust the strategic guidance that informs the PLA's defense posture, force deployments, contingency planning, and plans for force modernization.[3] Changes in the PLA's strategic guidance are driven by changes in its assessment of the security threats facing China and/or changes in the types of war the PLA must be prepared to fight. As China's interests have expanded, both geographically and into new domains, the country faces new threats to its national security. According to the 2015 defense white paper, the overall world situation continues to be peaceful for China, but "new threats from hegemonism, power politics and neo-interventionism" have emerged, and "international competition for the redistribution of power, rights and interests is tending to intensify."[4] According to the white paper, "The national security issues facing China encompass far more subjects, extend over a greater range, and cover a longer time span than at any time in the country's history." The white paper asserts that these issues include not only long-standing threats to China's sovereignty, such as the possibility that Taiwan will pursue independence and issues related to separatist forces in Xinjiang and Tibet, but also new threats to China's national security, such as the "rebalance" of U.S. military forces to Asia, Japan's improving military capabilities, and "provocative" actions taken by the Philippines and Vietnam over disputes in the South China Sea.[5]

While threats to its interests have expanded geographically, China also sees threats emerging in outer space and cyberspace. Indeed, space is described by the 2015 white paper as "a commanding height in international strategic competition." The white paper notes that certain

---

[1] See, for example, Kevin Pollpeter, "China's Space Doctrine," in Andrew S. Erickson and Lyle J. Goldstein, eds., *Chinese Aerospace Power,* Annapolis, Md.: Naval Institute Press, 2011, pp. 50–68.

[2] *China's Military Strategy*, The State Council Information Office of the People's Republic of China, Ministry of Defense, May 2015.

[3] David Finkelstein, "2015 Should Be an Exciting Year for PLA-Watching," *Pathfinder Magazine*, Vol. 13, No. 1, Winter 2015, p. 11.

[4] *China's Military Strategy*, 2015.

[5] *China's Military Strategy*, 2015.

countries "are developing their space forces" and that "the first signs of weaponization of outer space have appeared."[6]

To deal with these expanding security issues, the white paper states that China's military must be able to "safeguard China's security and interests in new domains," be able to deal with "a wide variety of emergencies and military threats," "prepare for military struggle in all directions and domains," and "will pay close attention to the challenges in new security domains, and work hard to seize the strategic initiative in military competition."[7] In regard to space, the white paper states that China "will keep abreast of the dynamics of outer space, deal with security threats and challenges in that domain, and secure its space assets to serve its national economic and social development, and maintain outer space security."[8]

The white paper also notes a change in the type of war the PLA must be prepared to fight. Since 1993, the evolution of the PLA's concept of modern war has captured the increasing importance of information to modern military operations. In 2004, the PLA's concept of war changed from "winning local wars in conditions of modern technology, particularly high technology" to "winning local wars under conditions of informatization." In 2015, this formulation was again changed to "winning informatized local wars." According to one military commentator, this new formulation indicates that "a qualitative change has occurred"[9] in a way that has substantially altered the PLA's thinking on the type of war it will fight. This latest formulation appears to emphasize, even more than previous formulations, the prominence of joint operations using networked information systems in all domains.[10]

Perhaps the most prominent feature of informatized local wars that differentiates this formulation from previous formulations is the concept of system-of-systems operations (SOSO). SOSO, also called "system-vs.-system warfare," has its roots in U.S. military writings on network-centric warfare and involves combat between systems of systems rather than between individual systems or platforms. According to the 2015 white paper, SOSO is intended to "accelerate operational response times to enhance firepower and maneuver, particularly by shortening and streamlining decision making and sensor to shooter times to get inside an opponent's decision cycle." SOSO "relies on information systems ... to unify and optimize force groupings, provide real-time information sharing and precision control of combat operations."[11] To carry out SOSO, the PLA is required to make "advances in communications, satellite

---

[6] *China's Military Strategy*, 2015.

[7] *China's Military Strategy*, 2015.

[8] *China's Military Strategy*, 2015.

[9] Guo Yuandan, "Want to Fight Naval Wars? China Should Prepare for Naval Combat" (要打海上战争？中国应做海上军事斗争准备), mil.huanqiu.com.

[10] Mu Zhiyong, "Paying Attention to the Construction of Integrated Information and Information System," *Study Times*, September 17, 2015.

[11] Kevin McCauley, "System of System Operational Capability: Key Supporting Concepts for Future Joint Operations," *China Brief*, October 5, 2012.

navigation, and reconnaissance capabilities that enable greater sharing of information, situational awareness, and a flatter command structure."[12]

But SOSO also places an emphasis on denying information to adversaries. Although Western analysts have for some time noted that the PLA has been following an asymmetric strategy to compensate for its weaknesses against the U.S. military, the 2013 *Science of Military Strategy* states that system-vs.-system operations are inherently asymmetric, regardless of the balance of forces. According to this logic, future conflicts between adversaries will be decided not only by the overall composition of a force, but also by its weaknesses and the ability of an adversary to strike those weaknesses to achieve decisive effects.[13] In fact, the 2013 *Science of Military Strategy* goes so far as to state that "local war under informatized conditions is system-vs.-system warfare" and that "in the future, no matter whether we will face an enemy with superior equipment or an enemy with inferior equipment, we will always need to focus on paralyzing enemy warfighting systems and emphasize 'striking at systems,' 'striking at vital sites,' and 'striking at [key] nodes',"[14] with the "most universal and practical" method of doing so being "asymmetrical operations."[15]

This emphasis on information systems is based on the requirement to conduct long-range joint operations. Although all services are tasked with modernization, the primary mission for the PLA is now defense of the maritime domain. According to the 2015 white paper, "The traditional mentality that land outweighs sea must be abandoned, and great importance has to be attached to managing the seas and oceans and protecting maritime rights and interests."[16] The white paper adds, "In line with the evolving form of war and national security situation, the basic point for preparation for military struggle will be placed on winning informatized local wars, highlighting maritime military struggle and maritime preparation for military struggle."[17]

Hand-in-hand with prioritization of the maritime domain is an emphasis on the new domains of space and cyber. Former President Hu Jintao, in his work report to the 18th Congress of the Chinese Communist Party in November 2012, ordered the PLA to "attach great importance" to maritime security, as well as to space and cyberspace security.[18] Just as the U.S. military had discovered, the farther a military ventures from its shores, the more attractive space becomes as a military domain. According to the 2013 *Science of Military Strategy*, PLA naval operations will involve a smaller forward-deployed force backed up by a main force stationed within Chinese

---

[12] McCauley, 2012.

[13] PLA Academy of Military Science (AMS) Military Strategy Studies Department, *Science of Military Strategy* （战略学）, Beijing: Military Science Press, December 2013, pp. 127–129.

[14] PLA Academy of Military Science (AMS) Military Strategy Studies Department, 2013, p. 126.

[15] PLA Academy of Military Science (AMS) Military Strategy Studies Department, 2013, p. 129.

[16] *China's Military Strategy*, 2015.

[17] *China's Military Strategy*, 2015.

[18] "Full Text of Hu Jintao's Report at 18th Party Congress," *Xinhua*, November 17, 2012.

territory or Chinese territorial waters tasked with conducting long-range strikes.[19] This new direction toward maritime operations stresses the use of long-range cruise and ballistic missiles, C4ISR systems to locate and track targets and provide communication between units, and information systems to process and disseminate intelligence. These types of operations require not only sensors such as over-the-horizon radar, but also space-based sensors and the information systems to process and transmit the intelligence collected by these sensors. In effect, space-based C4ISR provides a vital element of the connective tissue identified by SOSO needed for long-range joint operations that requires the PLA to both defend its space assets and threaten the space assets of potential adversaries. Thus, the 2015 white paper's characterization of space as a "commanding height of strategic competition" is based on the inherent role of space in PLA asymmetric operations, i.e., enabling long-range precision strikes through the use of space-based C4ISR capabilities and through counterspace operations that seek to deny an adversary the use of space.

---

[19] PLA Academy of Military Science (AMS) Military Strategy Studies Department, 2013, p. 108.

3. The Role of Outer Space in PLA Operations

The role space plays in enabling long-range precision strikes and in denying other militaries the use of C4ISR systems through counterspace operations is reflected in Chinese military writings on the use of space. As mentioned earlier, the concept of SOSO drives Chinese development of capabilities to ensure the PLA's ability to both use space for informatized warfare and degrade, disrupt, or deny adversary use of space. According to Chinese sources, the goal of space operations is to achieve space superiority (制天权), defined as "ensuring one's ability to fully use space while at the same time limiting, weakening, and destroying an adversary's space forces."[20] Chinese military analysts often assert that space is the ultimate high ground and that whoever controls space controls the earth. According to Chinese sources, the U.S. military uses satellites for 100 percent of its navigation needs, 80–90 percent of its communication needs, and 70–90 percent of its intelligence needs.[21] Many of these same sources also assert that China must follow the U.S. military's lead in its reliance on space. According to the *Textbook for the Study of Space Operations*, published by the PLA's most important think tank, the Academy of Military Science (AMS), "Whoever is the strongman of military space will be the ruler of the battlefield; whoever has the advantage of space has the power of the initiative; having 'space' support enables victory, lacking 'space' ensures defeat."[22]

The analysts at the AMS also conclude that although space is a great asset, reliance on space creates vulnerabilities that, if denied to an adversary, can create the conditions for victory. These analysts argue that at the same time the PLA needs to utilize space-based C4ISR technologies, it needs to develop countermeasures to deny these technologies to an adversary.[23] In fact, denying an adversary the use of space is deemed vital by two important Chinese texts. The 2013 *Science of Military Strategy* predicts that future wars may begin in outer space and cyberspace and that "achieving space superiority and cyber superiority are critical for achieving overall superiority and being victorious over an enemy."[24] The authors of the *Textbook for the Study of Space Operations* go even further and recommend that the PLA should "strive to attack first at the

---

[20] Jiang Lianju and Wang Liwen, eds., *Textbook for the Study of Space Operations* (空间作战靴教程), Beijing: Military Science Publishing House, 2013, p. 6.

[21] Jiang Lianju and Wang Liwen, eds., 2013, p. 150; PLA Academy of Military Science (AMS) Military Strategy Studies Department, 2013, p. 96; Chang Xianqi, *Military Astronautics* (军事航天学), Beijing: National Defense Industry Press, 2002, pp. 257–258.

[22] Jiang Lianju and Wang Liwen, eds., 2013, p. 1.

[23] See, for example, Jiang Lianju and Wang Liwen, eds., 2013, p. 127; and Chang Xianqi, 2002, p. 260.

[24] PLA Academy of Military Science (AMS) Military Strategy Studies Department, 2013, p. 96.

campaign and tactical levels in order to maintain the space battlefield initiative."[25] They also argue that fighting a quick war with a quick resolution is one of the "special characteristics of space operations" and that a military should "conceal the concentration of its forces and make a decisive large-scale first strike."[26]

China's Space-Based C4ISR Capabilities

China's space-based C4ISR capabilities provide what is called by some PLA sources "space information support" (空间信息支援) or what the U.S. Air Force (USAF) calls "force enhancement." It involves space-based intelligence, surveillance, and reconnaissance (ISR), communication, and navigation capabilities to support operations in other domains. Space information support is described as the basis of military space operations, with conflict in space revolving around the ability of a military to deny an adversary support from space-based assets.[27]

Since 2000, China has been rapidly modernizing its space-based C4ISR capabilities and has increased the number of its satellites from just a handful in 2000 to 181 by mid-2016, exceeded only by the United States.[28] By 2020, the country plans to establish a global, 24-hour, all-weather earth remote sensing system and a global satellite navigation system. By mid-2016, China had 76 operational remote sensing satellites in orbit, with six new types of remote sensing satellites having been launched since 2000: the Yaogan, Gaofen, Huanjing, Haiyang, Jilin, and Tianhui (see Table 3.1). These satellites provide a variety of sensors with a variety of resolutions, including electronic intelligence, electro-optical sensors, synthetic aperture radar, staring camera, and stereoscopic imagers.

China's satellite navigation system has also experienced tremendous progress. Following the establishment of a two-satellite regional navigation system in 2000, China has launched 22 navigation satellites. Although the system is still regional in its scope, China plans to have a global, 35-satellite constellation by 2020. The system offers accuracies of 5 meters that can be improved to better than 1 meter with the aid of ground-segment augmentation.

In addition to earth remote sensing and satellite navigation, China also has 34 civil, military, and commercial communication satellites. These include three Tianlian satellites designed to relay information between other satellites and ground stations. Ostensibly to eliminate communication blackouts for China's human space-flight program, these satellites can also be used to transmit information from remote sensing satellites back to ground stations.

---

[25] Jiang Lianju and Wang Liwen, eds., 2002, p. 5.

[26] Jiang Lianju and Wang Liwen, eds., 2002, pp. 142–143.

[27] PLA Academy of Military Science (AMS) Military Strategy Studies Department, 2013, p. 181.

[28] Union of Concerned Scientists, *UCS Satellite Database: In-Depth Details on the 1,459 Satellites Currently Orbiting Earth*, undated, last revised April 11, 2017.

Table 3.1. Chinese Remote Sensing Satellites Launched Since 2000

Satellite	Payload	Resolution	Number Operational (December 31, 2015)
Yaogan	EO, SAR, ELINT	1–10 m	29
Gaofen	EO, staring camera	EO = <1 m–2 m, 800 m; Staring camera = 50 m	5
Haiyang	EO and color scanners	EO = 250 m	1
Huanjing	EO	30 m	3
Jilin	EO	0.72 m	4
Tianhui	Stereoscopic	5 m	3

SOURCES: "Long March 3B Lofts Gaofen-4 to Close Out 2015," NASASpaceFlight.com, December 28, 2015; "China's Ocean Satellites" (中国海洋卫星), *Aerospace China* (中国航天), No. 372, April 2009, pp. 10–11; Wang Qiao, Wu Chuanqing, and Li Qing, "Environment Satellite 1 and Its Application in Environmental Monitoring," *Journal of Remote Sensing*, Vol. 1, 2010, p. 104; Rui C. Barbosa, "China Launches Jilin-1 Mission via Long March 2D," NASASpaceFlight.com, October 7, 2015. Note that NASASpaceFlight.com is not an official NASA website, but it provides valuable open source news and information resources on space developments.
NOTE: EO = electro-optical; SAR = synthetic aperture radar; ELINT = electronic intelligence.

Counterspace Capabilities

China has a wide-ranging counterspace program that includes kinetic-energy, directed-energy, co-orbital, EW, and cyber weapon programs that appear intended to threaten an adversary's space assets from the ground to geosynchronous orbit. China's counterspace capabilities are used to conduct what the PLA calls "space attack and defense operations" (空间攻防). This concept is roughly analogous to the USAF counterspace mission, but it also includes what the USAF defines as force application missions involving strikes by space-based platforms against terrestrial and airborne targets. The objective of PLA space attack and defense operations is to achieve space superiority within a certain period of time and at a certain location.[29] It includes offensive and defensive counterspace operations both between space-based platforms and between space and ground and air platforms.[30]

The most visible aspect of China's counterspace program is its kinetic-energy weapons program. Since its 2007 ASAT test that destroyed a retired meteorological satellite, China has conducted a number of non-debris-producing counterspace-related direct-ascent tests. These include ballistic missile defense tests in 2010 and 2013 and a counterspace test in 2014. The systems tested threaten satellites in low earth orbit such as remote sensing platforms, but in 2013 China conducted a so-called "high-altitude science mission" that the U.S. Department of Defense

---

[29] PLA Academy of Military Science (AMS) Military Strategy Studies Department, 2013, p. 182.

[30] PLA Academy of Military Science (AMS) Military Strategy Studies Department, 2013, p. 182.

9

assessed to be a counterspace test designed to reach satellites in geosynchronous orbit.[31] With this system, China could have the capability to attack satellites in higher orbits such as Global Positioning System (GPS) and communication satellites.

China has also conducted a number of co-orbital tests with counterspace implications. In a 2010 test, two Shijian satellites reportedly bumped into each other. Neither the Chinese government nor the military commented on the nature of the test, but the maneuver could have been a test run for the first docking of a Shenzhou space capsule with the Tiangong-1 space station, conducted in 2011.[32] However, the silence of the Chinese government about the test raised concerns about its counterspace implications. A 2013 test raised similar concerns when three Chinese satellites conducted close-proximity operations involving one satellite grabbing another with a robotic arm.[33] In June 2016, China again launched a satellite, Aolong-1, equipped with a robotic arm that is purportedly intended to remove space debris.[34] In the same month, China launched a satellite to test in-orbit refueling capabilities, which also involve co-orbital capabilities.[35]

China has reportedly been implicated in two cyber intrusions that targeted U.S. space facilities (see Table 3.2). An intrusion against the Jet Propulsion Laboratory was said to have resulted in the perpetrators gaining full control over the laboratory's computer networks.[36] Reports of a Chinese intrusion involving the National Oceanic and Atmospheric Administration lack many details, including information about the type or severity of the incident.[37] China is also pursuing directed-energy weapons for use against satellites. In 2006, a Chinese laser painted a U.S. reconnaissance satellite, inflicting no permanent damage. The intent of the lasing is unknown, however, and could have been the result of the Chinese attempting to range the satellite rather than interfere with its operation.[38]

---

[31] Office of the Secretary of Defense, *Annual Report to Congress: Military and Security Developments Involving the People's Republic of China 2015*, U.S. Department of Defense, 2015, p. 13.

[32] Rui C. Barbosa, "China's Shenzhou 9 Successfully Docks with Tiangong-1," NASASpaceFlight.com, June 18, 2012.

[33] Brian Weeden, "Dancing in the Dark: The Orbital Rendezvous of SJ-12 and SJ-06F," *Space Review*, August 30, 2010; and Kevin Pollpeter, "China's Space Robotic Arm Programs," *SITC News Analysis,* October 2013.

[34] "China's New Orbital Debris Clean-Up Satellite Raises Space Militarization Concerns," Spaceflight101.com, June 29, 2016.

[35] "China Announces Success in Technology to Refuel Satellites in Orbit," *Xinhua*, June 30, 2016.

[36] Paul K. Martin, Inspector General, National Aeronautics and Space Administration, "NASA Cyber Security: An Examination of the Agency's Information Security," Testimony Before the Subcommittee on Investigations and Oversight, House Committee on Science, Space, and Technology, February 29, 2012, p. 5.

[37] Mary Pat Flaherty, Jason Samenow, and Lisa Rein, "Chinese Hack U.S. Weather Systems, Satellite Network," *Washington Post*, November 12, 2014.

[38] Elaine M. Grossman, "Top Commander: Chinese Interference with U.S. Satellites Uncertain," *World Politics Review,* October 18, 2006.

Table 3.2. Chinese Counterspace Operations and Tests, Including Tests with Counterspace Implications

Year	Technology
	Directed Energy
2006	Chinese laser reportedly paints U.S. satellite
	Kinetic Energy
2007	China destroys FY-1C meteorological satellite with direct-ascent KKV
2010	China conducts midcourse ballistic missile defense test
2013	China conducts direct-ascent KKV test to GEO
2013	China conducts midcourse ballistic missile defense test
2014	China conducts direct-ascent KKV test
2015	KKV test of undeclared purpose
	Co-orbital
2010	Two Shijian satellites involved in close proximity operation
2013	Three satellites involved in close proximity operation to test robotic arm technologies
2016	Launch of satellite equipped with robotic arm for space debris removal
2016	Launch of satellite to test in-orbit refueling technologies
	Cyber
2012	Cyber intrusion reported against Jet Propulsion Laboratory
2014	Cyber intrusion reported against National Oceanic and Atmospheric Administration

SOURCE: This is a modified version of a table that appears in Kevin Pollpeter, Eric Anderson, and Fan Yang, *China Dream, Space Dream: China's Progress in Space Technologies and Implications for the United States*, Institute on Global Conflict and Cooperation, March 2015, p. 86.
NOTE: KKV = kinetic kill vehicles; GEO = geostationary earth orbit.

Finally, China has focused considerable resources on developing capabilities to jam satellite communications and navigation-satellite signals. Navigation satellites are particularly vulnerable to jamming because of their weak signal.[39]

---

[39] Office of the Secretary of Defense, *Annual Report to Congress: Military and Security Developments Involving the People's Republic of China 2011*, U.S. Department of Defense, 2011, p. 37.

4. The Strategic Support Force

It is against this background of space's growing importance to PLA operations that we begin to explore the organizational structure of the PLA's space program. As China has improved and expanded its space and counterspace capabilities, calls have come from some in China's space community to organize China's space program under an executive agent. According to prominent engineers in China's space program, the existence of too many organizations under different chains of command has hindered the ability of the space program to respond to crises such as the 2008 Wenchuan earthquake.[40]

Chinese military analysts have discussed reorganizing the command structure of China's space program, with some lobbying for leadership to be undertaken by their particular service. The most vociferous of these proponents have been analysts from the PLA Air Force (PLAAF). These analysts have argued that the PLAAF is the most technical of the branches and thus the best service to take on and understand space technologies. Their second argument characterized the future of military space as lying with manned platforms, such space planes. According to this argument, the PLAAF, with its responsibility for manned aircraft, is the best service to take on this mission. A third argument is that the air forces of other militaries command space programs, and the PLAAF should be no different.[41] However, a different vision for the PLAAF was set out in the 2013 *Science of Military Strategy*. In that vision, the PLAAF's space role would be mainly as a consumer of space-derived information, but at some time in the future, as space planes, air-launched ASAT weapons, and airborne lasers become more developed, the PLAAF would play a more prominent role in China's space program.[42]

A second service that has stated an interest in China's space program is the PLA Rocket Force (previously the PLA Second Artillery Force). According to one internal source on missile campaigns, the Rocket Force would play an important role in space operations.[43] While seemingly downplaying the role of the PLAAF in space operations, the 2013 *Science of Military Strategy* foresees a more prominent role for the Rocket Force. The text describes it as inherently a space organization because ballistic missile warheads travel through space to reach their

---

[40] "Scientists: China Should Integrate Space Resources to Improve Emergency Response," *People's Daily Online*, March 4, 2009.

[41] For more on PLAAF analysts' views on space, see Kevin Pollpeter, "The PLAAF and the Integration of Air and Space Power," in Richard P. Hallion, Roger Cliff, and Phillip C. Saunders, *The Chinese Air Force: Evolving Concepts, Roles, and Capabilities*, Washington, D.C.: National Defense University Press, 2012, pp. 165–190.

[42] PLA Academy of Military Science (AMS) Military Strategy Studies Department, 2013, pp. 223–224.

[43] Yu Jixun, ed., *Science of Second Artillery Campaigns* (第二炮兵战役学), Beijing: National Defense University Press, 2004, pp. 70 and 142.

targets. The *Science of Military Strategy* also notes that with little effort, ballistic missiles can be modified into launch vehicles or direct-ascent ASAT launchers.[44]

This lobbying, however, appears to have failed. China's military leadership decided not to transfer the space program to one of the services and instead transferred it to an entirely new organization, the SSF. And instead of forming an organization dedicated solely to the space mission, the PLA merged the space mission with the EW and cyber missions under the umbrella of the SSF.

In this chapter, we discuss the creation of the SSF, with the assumption that any understanding of the PLA's space program must be embedded in an understanding of the organizational structure of the SSF. With the creation of the SSF, the PLA has highlighted the importance of not only space operations but also information operations of all types and the need to bring the PLA's information-warfare units under a single command. Indeed, the creation of the SSF appears to be an outcome of the "decisions" of the Third Plenum of the 18th Chinese Communist Party Congress to improve "the leadership of new type combat forces."[45]

The creation of the SSF on December 31, 2015, was part of a larger series of reforms intended to streamline the PLA to make it better able to respond to contingencies and make it a more effective fighting force by providing a force structure that better enables joint operations. These reforms not only established the Ground Force as a separate service and replaced the Second Artillery with the Rocket Force, but also replaced the four general departments—the GSD, the General Political Department (GPD), the General Logistics Department (GLD), and the GAD—with 15 functional departments, offices, and commissions; it also abolished the former regional command system made up of seven ground-force-dominated military regions (MRs) and replaced them with five joint theater commands. Due to be completed by 2020, these reforms are intended to establish a system in which the "CMC [Central Military Commission] is in overall command, the theater commands fight war, and the services build forces" (军委管总、战区主战、军种主建).[46]

Despite the importance of the SSF, very little official information has been released on its missions and makeup. According to Chinese President Xi Jinping, the SSF is a "new type operational force to maintain national security" and "an important growth point" for the PLA's "new quality operational capability." During the organization's inauguration ceremony, Xi encouraged the SSF's officer corps to persist in system integration (体系融合) and civil-military integration (军民融合) while carrying out the mission of the SSF, as well as "to work hard to

---

[44] PLA Academy of Military Science (AMS) Military Strategy Studies Department, 2013, pp. 229–230.

[45] "Decision of the Central Committee of the Communist Party of China on Some Major Issues Concerning Comprehensively Deepening the Reform," *Xinhua*, January 16, 2014.

[46] "The CMC's Opinions on Deepening National Defense and Military Reform" (中央军委关于深化国防和军队改革的意见 (全文)), January 1, 2016.

14

achieve leap frog development in key areas" and "jointly develop and work hard to build a powerful modern Strategic Support Force."[47]

According to a Ministry of National Defense spokesperson, the SSF was founded to provide "strong strategic, foundational, and sustainment support to carry out the integration of capabilities." The spokesperson also stated that the SSF would "optimize the structure of the military forces and improve comprehensive support capabilities."[48]

Beyond this, little official information has been released, leading the author of one Chinese article to call the force "mysterious."[49] Other sources have provided additional information on the SSF, however. According to an article appearing on the official *China Military Online* website, the SSF is an important component of joint operations that supports battlefield operations by providing information and strategic support to form an "information umbrella" for other services.[50] In addition, an article appearing in the *Liberation Army Daily* associates the SSF with space and cyber: "In order to meet the requirements of building a strong space power and a strong cyber power, the Strategic Support Force was established to create a new type operational force that can protect the country's security."[51]

According to an interview with retired admiral and head of the Naval Network Security and Informatization Expert Advisory Committee Yin Zhuo that first appeared on the *People's Daily* website but was then posted on the Ministry of National Defense website, the SSF is an important component of joint operations.[52] Yin stated that the mission of the SSF is to provide support to the battlefield so that the PLA can achieve superiority in the space, cyberspace, and electromagnetic domains. He said that the SSF is not an independent operational force and instead described it as "an important force in joint operations whose actions will be integrated with the Army, Navy, Air Force, and Rocket Force." According to Yin, the mission of the SSF is

[47] Wang Shibin and An Puzhong, "Xi Jinping Confers Military Flags to Chinese People's Liberation Army Ground Force, Rocket Force, and Strategic Rocket Force" (习近平向中国人民解放军陆军火箭军战略支援部队授予军旗并致训词), *China Military Net* (中国军网), January 1, 2016.

[48] Ren Xu, "Ministry of National Defense Spokesperson Takes Media Inquiries on Deepening National Defense and Military Reform" (国防部新闻发言人就深化国防和军队改革有关问题接受媒体专访), *China Military Net* (中国军网), January 1, 2016.

[49] Qiu Yue, "Our Military's Strategic Support Force Is What Type of Military Force?" (我军战略支援部队是一支什么样的军事力量？), *China Military Online* (中国军网), January 5, 2016.

[50] Ni Guanghui, "Our Military's Secretive First Strategic Support Force" (揭秘我军首支战略支援部队), *China Military Online* (中国军网), January 24, 2016.

[51] "The Reader for Chairman Xi Jinping's Important Expositions on National Defense and Military Reform (2016 Edition) on Resolutely Winning the Battle to Deepen National Defense and Military Reform – On Completely Implementing the Strategy on Reforming and Strengthening the Military" (习主席国防和军队建设重要论述读本（2016年版）坚决打赢深化国防和军队改革这场攻坚战—关于全面实施改革强军战略), *Liberation Army Daily* (解放军报), May 26, 2016, p. 4.

[52] "Expert: The Strategic Support Force Will Be Critical for Victory During the Entire Operation" (专家:战略支援部队将贯穿作战全过程 是致胜关键), *People's Daily Online* (人民网), January 5, 2016.

to provide ISR and navigation support. In doing so, the SSF will manage navigation and reconnaissance satellites in addition to defending the cyber and electromagnetic domains.[53]

Former Second Artillery officer Song Zhongping, however, contends that the SSF is an independent service "unique in the world" and that the concept of the SSF puts the PLA ahead of the U.S. military in organizing its information-warfare forces. According to Song, whereas the U.S. military inefficiently disperses its information-warfare forces among the services, the SSF concentrates the PLA's information-warfare forces under one command. He adds that the SSF is made up of a cyber force composed of network attack and defense units, a space force mainly responsible for reconnaissance and navigation satellites, and EW units responsible for countering enemy radar and communications. Song states that the goal of the SSF is to achieve cyber and electromagnetic superiority, but he does not mention space superiority as a goal. He also states that the PLAAF will transfer its space functions, including the operation of the Shenlong space plane, to the SSF, but that the PLAAF will retain its missile defense and counterspace functions. In the same article, Du Songtao, another military commentator, states that the SSF is composed of units from the GSD, the GAD, and the GLD.[54]

Finally, the authors of an article appearing on an unofficial Chinese website that frequently covers military topics characterized the PLA as now being made up of three levels of services: the three traditional services—the Army, Air Force, and Navy; a second level, the Rocket Force; and a third level, a "space-cyber force" (天-网军). The article describes the SSF as being made up of space, cyber, EW, and psychological warfare units and being responsible for satellite operations.[55]

The lack of authoritative sources on the composition, missions, and command of the SSF reflects China's opacity about many aspects of its military space activities. It may also suggest that as the PLA is still in a relatively early stage of a major reorganization, aspects of it remain works in progress, and the PLA can be expected to make further changes or refinements as it moves ahead with the reforms and tests them in military exercises or operations.

Organization and Leadership

The SSF's apparent responsibility for space, cyber, and EW missions is supported by considerable data collected on its organization and leadership. Despite Chinese opacity, we were able to piece together a number of elements of SSF organization and leadership based on official

---

[53] Qiu Yue, 2016.

[54] "Expert Says the Strategic Support Force Independently Becomes a Military Concept Ahead of the U.S. Military" (专家称战略支援部队独立成军 理念领先于美军) ,sina.com, January 8, 2016.

[55] "The Strategic Support Force Is Actually a Space-Cyber Force: It Will Change Warfare" (战略支援部队其实就是天网军：将改变战争), war.163.com, November 1, 2015. While 163.com is certainly not an official, authoritative source, the website remains a useful provider of open-source information on Chinese military and security developments.

and semiofficial PLA publications, postings on Chinese government space and technology websites, and other publicly available Chinese-language sources.

For example, a four-page spread on the SSF in *PLA Pictorial* featuring space- and EW-related photos indicates that the SSF's mission at a minimum involves space and EW.[56] Indeed, the SSF appears to be made up of units drawn exclusively from the GSD and GAD, as well as new units created to carry out its mission. The two new units are the Space Systems Department (航天系统部)[57] to carry out the SSF's space missions and the Network Systems Department (网络系统部)[58] to carry out the SSF's cyber and EW missions. Space-related units in the Space Systems Department include launch centers and satellite control centers from the former GAD. Other units within the SSF include research institutes from the former GSD[59] and could also include units from the Third and Fourth Departments of the former GSD responsible for signals intelligence and electronic countermeasures and radar, respectively, as well as the Informatization Department, which is responsible for communications.[60]

The SSF's organizational structure is reflected in an officer corps drawn heavily from the space program and Ground Force (see Table 4.1). According to official sources, the SSF is led by commander Lieutenant General (LTG) (中将) Gao Jin and political commissar (PC) General (上将) Liu Fulian. LTG Gao is a former Second Artillery officer who became the Second Artillery chief of staff in 2011. In 2014, he became an aide to the chief of the General Staff and then the commandant of the AMS. Born in 1959, Gao is the youngest officer to have become an MR-grade officer and the youngest commandant of the AMS.[61] General Liu Fulian, on the other hand, has spent his entire career in or around Beijing. He was previously the PC for the 27th

---

[56] Yang Yunfang, "The Strategic Support Force Joint Victory" (战略支援部队新型战力联合制胜), *PLA Pictorial* (解放军报), No. 935, 2016/1, pp. 32–35.

[57] "Announcement of Tender for New Space Electronic Equipment" (航天装备新品电子元器件科研项目招标公告), All Military Weapons and Equipment Purchasing Information Network (全军武器装备采购信息网), August 4, 2016. The source is the Central Military Commission Equipment Development Department (中央军委装备发展部), the PLA entity in charge of equipment development and design under the latest PLA reforms.

[58] "Class-A Qualification List for Integrated Information System" (涉密信息系统集成甲级资质单位名录), National Secrecy Science and Technology Evaluation Center (国家保密科技测评中心), November 18, 2016. The National Secrecy Science and Technology Evaluation Center (国家保密科技测评中心) is a Chinese government entity in charge of protecting Chinese science and technology information security.

[59] "China PLA Strategic Support Force Network Systems Department 56th Research Institute" (中国人民解放军战略支援部队网络系统部第五十六研究所), China Graduate Student Enrollment Information Network, May 24, 2017; and "China PLA GSD 58th Research Institute (中国人民解放军总参第五十八研究所), China Graduate Student Enrollment Information Network, September 13, 2016.

[60] "Laser Ranging Systems Project Sole Source Announcement (激光探测定位系统项目单一来源采购公示公告), Beijing Guotai Jianzhong Management and Consulting Co. Ltd., October 31, 2016; and "Partial List of Expert Report Topics," *Journal of Radars*, Excel spreadsheet, undated.

[61] "Gao Jin Becomes PLA's Youngest Military Region-Level Chief," *Want China Times*, December 25, 2014.

17

Table 4.1. SSF Leadership

Name	Position	Grade/Rank
Gao Jin (高津)	Commander	MR/LTG
Liu Fulian (刘福连)	PC	MR/General
Liu Shangfu (刘尚福)	Deputy Commander/Chief of Staff	MR Deputy Leader/Major General
Rao Kaixun (饶开勋)	Deputy Commander	Corps Leader/Major General
Lu Jiancheng (吕建成)	Deputy PC	MR Deputy Leader/LTG
Feng Jianhua (冯建华)	Head of Disciplinary Inspection Committee	MR Deputy Leader/Major General
Shang Hong (尚宏)	Commander, Space Systems Department	MR Deputy Leader/Major General
Kang Chunyuan (康春元)	PC, Space Systems Department	MR Deputy Leader/Major General
Zheng Junjie (郑俊杰)	Commander, Network Systems Department	MR Deputy Leader/Major General
Chai Liangshao (柴绍良)	PC, Network Systems Department	MR Deputy Leader/LTG

Group Army based in the Beijing MR, was the PC for the Beijing Garrison, and before his appointment to the SSF was the PC for the Beijing MR. [62]

Official and unofficial sources describe a second level of leadership below the commander and PC composed of former Launch Center commanders and Ground Force officers. Major General Liu Shangfu has been officially identified as a deputy commander and chief of staff of the SSF.[63] Liu was formerly the commander of the Xichang Satellite Launch Center, deputy

---

[62] "Beijing MR Political Commissar Liu Fulian Biography" (北京军区政委刘福连简历, *Ta Kong Pao*, July 31, 2013.

[63] "The Third Stage of the Lunar Exploration Project Chang'e 5 Transitions to the Final Research and Development Stage" (探月三期嫦娥五号任务转入正样研制阶段), State Administration for Science and Technology and Industry for National Defense, February 19, 2016.

commander of the human spaceflight program, the GAD chief of staff, and most recently, a GAD deputy commander.[64]

For other members of this second tier of leadership, we must rely on unofficial reporting. Major General Rao Kaixun, a former Ground Force officer who was the GSD Operations Department commander, is a deputy commander.[65] Reported deputy PC LTG Lu Jiancheng has spent his career in a variety of posts, most recently as deputy PC for the Jinan MR. Major General Feng Jianhua is reportedly the head of the SSF's Disciplinary Inspection Committee and the director of the organization's Political Department. He has also been identified as the former head of the GPD Cadre Department and the former deputy director of the GAD Political Department.[66]

Additional members of the leadership team are the commanders and PCs for the SSF's Space Systems Department and the Network Systems Department. The commander of the Space Systems Department is reportedly Major General Shang Hong, who was formerly the director of the Jiuquan Launch Center.[67] Its PC is reportedly Major General Kang Chunyuan, a former Ground Force officer and the former deputy PC for the Lanzhou MR.[68] The reported commander of the Network System Department is Major General Zheng Junjie. Zheng was formerly the deputy director of the GSD Third Department, responsible for signals intelligence, and the former commandant of the PLA Information Engineering University.[69] The PC of the Network Systems Department is reportedly LTG Chai Liangshao, who was formerly a *mishu* (secretary) for the GPD, the director of the GPD Organization Department, the director of the Chengdu MR Political Department, and a deputy PC for the GAD.[70]

---

[64] "The Scoop: Two Major Generals Become Commanders of the Strategic Support Force" (独家报道：两少将任战略支援部队副司令) ,*Da Gong Bao* (大公报), January 6, 2016.

[65] "The Scoop: Two Major Generals Become Commanders of the Strategic Support Force," 2016.

[66] "Major General Feng Jianhua Will Transfer to Be Strategic Support Force Political Department Director" (冯建华少将调任战略支援部队政治部主任), news.sohu.com, February 28, 2016.

[67] "Liu Fulian Becomes Deputy Commander and Chief of Staff of the Strategic Support Force" (李尚福任战略支援部队副司令员兼参谋长(图)), Huanqiu.com, February 9, 2016.

[68] "Members of the Strategic Support Force Leadership Group Including Space Force and Cyber Force Commanders and PCs Generals for the Four General Departments Take Positions" (战略支援部队首任领导班子成员 包括天军网军司令政委 四总部将领履新), blog.sina.cn, January 8, 2016.

[69] "General Staff Personnel Changes Wang Huiqing Becomes Strategic Planning Department Director Zheng Junie Becomes Third Department Director" (总参人事变动王辉青任战略规划部部长郑俊杰任三部), 163.com, November 1, 2015.

[70] Wang Jun, "Chengdu MR Political Department Director Liang Chaishao Changes Positions to Become MR Deputy PC" (成都军区政治部主任柴绍良改任军区副政委), *Dagong Bao* (大公报), December 31, 2013.

Below this level are additional space- and cyber-related units. Former PC of the Jiuquan Launch Center[71] Wang Zhaoyu, for example, has been identified as a "former PC of a certain Strategic Support Force base."[72] National People's Congress military representative Chu Hongbin, identified as the PC of an unidentified SSF unit,[73] was identified in 2014 as the PC of an unidentified GAD unit involved with providing telemetry, tracking, and control for China's space program.[74] A third article identifies Chinese Academy of Sciences (CAS) Academician Zhou Zhixin as the bureau chief of a "certain Strategic Support Force bureau."[75] Zhou had previously been identified as director of the Beijing Institute for Remote Sensing,[76] also known as the GSD Space Technology Research Bureau, a unit subordinate to the GSD Second Department Technology Bureau.[77]

The SSF also contains at least one former GSD research institute. The *Liberation Army Daily* website carried an article by Tang Shuhai of a "certain Strategic Support Force research institute."[78] Tang was previously listed as a member of a "certain GSD research institute."[79] The former GSD 56th Research Institute has also been identified as being within the SSF's Network Systems Department.[80]

Further information about the leadership and organization of the SSF was revealed during President Xi's visit to SSF headquarters in what appears to be the former GAD headquarters building. A China Central Television report of Xi's visit showed a headquarters staff made up

[71] "Wang Jun Meets Wang Zhaoyu, Liu Jianguo, and Han Qiang" (王君会见王兆宇刘建国韩强), CCP [National Congress of the Communist Party of China] Information Network (中国共产党信息网), February 21, 2013.

[72] An Puzhong, Ouyang Hao, and Du Kang, "Keeping a Clean Political Environment – Military NPC Representatives Eager Building Work Style" (永葆绿水青山的政治生态—军队人大代表热议作风建设), *China Military Online* (中国军网), March 10, 2016.

[73] Zou Weirong, "Military NPC Representatives View the Pace of a Strong and Rejuvenated Military (军队人大代表眼中的强军兴军步伐), *People's Daily Online* (人民网), March 15, 2016.

[74] Wang Shibin, Yin Hang, and Song Xin, "The Best Is to Have a Motivated Heart: Sidelights of President Xi Jinping Meeting with Parts of the Grassroots NPC Representatives (最是深情励军心 -习近平主席接见部分军队基层人大代表侧记), *Liberation Reporter* (解放记者), March 12, 2014.

[75] "Adhere to Innovation Driven Development Promote Military Innovation Capabilities" (坚持创新驱动发展 提升军事创新能力), Ministry of National Defense website, April 4, 2016.

[76] Academic Divisions of the Chinese Academy of Sciences, homepage, undated.

[77] Mark Stokes and Ian Easton, "The Chinese People's Liberation Army General Staff Department: Evolving Organization and Missions," in Kevin Pollpeter and Kenneth W. Allen, eds., *PLA as Organization V2.0*, Vienna, Va.: Defense Group, Inc., 2015, p. 146.

[78] "Liberation Army Daily: Form Unique Advantages in R&D Competition" （解放军报：在科研必争领域形成独特优势）, CCP Information Network (中国共产党信息网), March 22, 2016.

[79] "Nie Rongzhen Feared Corrupt S&T Cadres: Early On Checked Them Individually" （聂荣臻怕科技干部冻坏手：早上出操挨个查看), Ecns (中国新闻网), January 28, 2015.

[80] "Class-A Qualification List for Integrated Information System," 2016.

primarily of Army officers but also including Navy and Air Force personnel. No Rocket Force officers were observed in the video.[81] Identified officers are listed in Table 4.2.

Table 4.2. Some Identified SSF Officers

Name	Name (Chinese)	Position	Former Organization
Wan Minggui	万明贵	Director	GAD Political Department
Chen Jinrong	陈金荣	Director	GAD Political Department
Xiao Zifeng	肖子峰	Deputy director	GAD Political Department
Hu Yuhai	胡瑜海	Deputy director	GAD Organization Department
Zhang Zhihui	张志辉	Deputy director	GSD Political Department
Cheng Jian	程坚	Deputy director	GSD Political Department
Yu Peijun	余培军	Deputy director	Xi'an Satellite Control Center
Sun Bo	孙波	Director	GSD Management Support Department
Lin Yu'nan	林玉南	Director	UI GAD Unit
Xia Xiaopeng	夏晓鹏	PC	Jiuquan Launch Center
Shang Hong	尚宏	Commander	Jiuquan Launch Center
Zou Lipeng	邹利鹏	Chief of staff	Jiuquan Launch Center
Yi Ziqian	易自谦	Deputy commander	Xichang Launch Center
Wu Weilin	吴卫林	PC	Taiyuan Launch Center
Wang Guoyu	王国玉	Deputy director	Electronic and Information Infrastructure Department
Feng Aiwang	冯爱旺	Deputy chief of staff	Headquarters Department, BJMRAF

SOURCE: "Xi Jinping Visits Strategic Support Force Organization Today," 2016.
NOTE: UI = Unidentified; BJMRAF = Beijing MR Air Force.

Understanding the SSF's Role and Composition

Given the lack of official information on the SSF, we can present only what we think about the role and composition of the SSF. In doing so, we not only sum up what we have learned from official and unofficial sources but also clarify our understanding of the SSF. This discussion relies, in part, on definitions found in the *Chinese People's Liberation Army Military Terminology* (hereafter referred to as *Military Terminology*), an official publication of the PLA intended to provide a common lexicon across the PLA, to illuminate the official characterizations of the SSF.

The first question that must be addressed in determining the role of the SSF is whether it is a service, as former Second Artillery officer Song Zhongping contends, or a force whose units will be integrated into the operations of the services, as retired Admiral Yin Zhuo claims. Force (or unit), translated as *budui* (部队), is defined by *Military Terminology* as a "(1) *Tuan*-level unit or

---

[81] "Xi Jinping Visits Strategic Support Force Organization Today," (习近平今日视察战略支援部队机关), *China News Online* (中国新闻网), August 29, 2016.

21

above that is directly responsible for an operational or support mission. (2) A part of a military. For example, troops located in Beijing, artillery units, and air force units. (3) A general term for a military."[82] A service (军种), on the other hand, is defined as "a main type of military division according to an important operational domain and combat arm."

Three factors appear to indicate that the SSF is not a service. First, and perhaps most convincingly, the PLA purposefully designated the SSF as a force and not a service, indicating that there is a real difference between the SSF and the designated services. The second factor is the composition of the SSF's office corps, which is dominated by Army officers, with a smaller contingent of Navy and Air Force officers. Indeed, no photos of SSF personnel show them wearing a separate SSF uniform, indicating that the SSF is a joint organization.[83]

The third factor consists of the definitions of *support* and *strategic support*. *Support* (支援) is defined as "weapons and forces under the direct command and subordinate to a certain unit that assists other units or neighboring operations."[84] *Strategic support*, in contrast, is defined as "support provided to other operational *jituan* (作战集团) units or the country in order to achieve a strategic goal." This support can come in the form of units, fire support, C4ISR capabilities, or logistics.[85] Operational *jituan* is defined here as "different forces involved in a campaign that are temporarily formed into a larger force to carry out an operational mission."[86]

Yin's characterization of the SSF as an augmentation force composed of space, cyber, and EW units is supported by these definitions. His characterization is also supported by an article appearing on the Central Theater Command website recounting a joint exercise involving personnel from the SSF who removed malware from a computer system and then conducted a cyber strike against the perpetrators. The SSF personnel also defended a Rocket Force unit from an EW attack.[87]

President Xi's call to persist in "system integration" (体系融合) in carrying forward the mission of the SSF is also suggestive of a support role for the organization. There is no definition of system integration in *Military Terminology*, but according to multiple sources, the term refers to a high degree of integration between command organizations, platforms, weapon systems, and information systems to form a complete and unitary operational force. System integration is based on the assessment that modern war is no longer decided by combat between platforms but is now a contest between opposing systems of warfare. It posits that those militaries that can best

---

[82] All-Army Military Terminology Management Committee, *Chinese People's Liberation Army Military Terminology* (中国人民解放军军语), Beijing: Military Science Press, 2011, p. 332.

[83] See, for example, "Xi Jinping Visits Strategic Support Force Organization Today," 2016.

[84] All-Army Military Terminology Management Committee, 2011, p. 86.

[85] All-Army Military Terminology Management Committee, 2011, p. 61.

[86] All-Army Military Terminology Management Committee, 2011, p. 65.

[87] "Rocket Force, Strategic Support Force Support Joint Readiness During the Spring Festival" (火箭军、战略支援部队等军种春节联合战备), *Liberation Reporter* (解放记者), February 10, 2016.

link platforms, weapon systems, and information systems and support operations with effective intelligence and a common battlefield picture will achieve victory.[88] System integration is closely related to the PLA's concept of system-vs.-system operations discussed earlier that emphasizes information dominance, precision strikes, and joint operations.

These definitions indicate that the SSF is not an independent force but instead is a force intended to augment service and theater command operations. The evidence does not support the contention made by former Second Artillery officer Song Zhongping that the SSF is a service. Nevertheless, the SSF can be expected to recruit, train, and equip its forces much like the services. Moreover, the actual missions of the SSF may at some point blur the distinction between a service and a force as it applies to the SSF. This assessment is based on two factors: (1) the definition of service as "a main type of military division according to an important operational domain"; and (2) the designation of outer space and cyberspace by the 2015 defense white paper as domains that "have become new commanding heights in strategic competition." SSF responsibilities for space and cyber missions would thus appear to indicate that the SSF is responsible for two "important operational domains" that would qualify it as a service. Although it appears unlikely that this is the case at the present time, it leaves open the possibility that as space and cyber warfare become more developed and have a greater potential to become independent campaigns, the SSF, like the Second Artillery, could become a full-fledged service.

This assessment appears to be buttressed by SSF commander Gao's position as an MR-grade officer, which places the SSF on a par bureaucratically with the services and the theater commands. In this respect, the SSF could be similar to the former Second Artillery, which, despite being a combat arm, was led by an MR-grade officer and treated as a service. It might also indicate that the SSF may gain representation on the Central Military Commission.[89]

Although the sources reviewed for this report do not support Song Zhongping's statement that the SSF is a service, they do support his characterization of the SSF as "unique in the world." While the SSF is neither a service nor a theater command, it does not appear to be like a unified command found in the U.S. military, such as the Strategic Command, which is also responsible for space and cyber. Whereas the U.S. military unified commands rely on the services for staffing and equipment, the SSF is organized around a force made up primarily of Army officers.[90]

---

[88] See, for example, Qin Lixin and Zhang Yi, "A Limited Definition of System Integration" (体系融合小意), Ministry of National Defense website, November 12, 2015; and Zhao Hui, "Problems of Joint Training Under the Information-Technology-Based Condition" (信息化条件下联合训练问题探析), *National Defense Science and Technology* (国防科技工业), Vol. 34, No. 1, February 2013, p. 79.

[89] The authors thank Ken Allen for this point.

[90] John Costello, "China Finally Centralizes Its Space, Cyber, Information Forces," *The Diplomat*, January 20, 2016.

5. The SSF's Organizational Structure for the Space Mission

The creation of the SSF is a major restructuring of the PLA's command system and an important step in fostering joint operations. To better understand how the SSF's organizational structure for the space mission differs from the organization of the space program in the pre-reform era and how this may affect space operations, we compare a proposed organizational structure of China's space program based on the evidence compiled to date with the organization of its space program before the creation of the SSF.

China's Pre-Reform Space Enterprise

China's pre-reform space enterprise was made up of a multitude of organizations spanning the military, government, and the defense industry.[91] China did not have an executive agent for space, such as some type of space command, nor did it appear to have an organization responsible for control of space assets during military operations, such as the U.S. military's Joint Functional Component Command for Space. The main component of China's space program was the GAD, which was responsible for the R&D of spacecraft and launch vehicles and the operation of launch centers and telemetry, tracking, and control (TT&C) facilities. These included the Beijing Aerospace Control Center, the Xi'an Satellite Control Center, and a number of domestically and internationally based TT&C ground stations and tracking and control ships, as well as four launch centers located in Jiuquan, Inner Mongolia; Taiyuan, Shanxi Province; Xichang, Sichuan Province; and Wenchang, Hainan Province. The GAD was also responsible for China's human spaceflight program under the China Manned Space Agency.[92]

In addition to the GAD, the GSD also played a role in space operations through a number of intelligence and EW units. These include

- The Intelligence Department (also known as the Second Department), which was responsible for intelligence collection and analysis. The Intelligence Department reportedly took on many of the characteristics of the U.S. National Reconnaissance Office with the PLA's increasing emphasis on the use of a space-based ISR system and its command of receiving stations for space-derived intelligence. These activities appear to have been carried out by the Intelligence Department's Aerospace Reconnaissance Bureaus.[93]

---

[91] For more on China's pre-reform space mission and organization, see Pollpeter, Anderson, and Fan, 2015.

[92] Pollpeter, Anderson, and Fan, 2015.

[93] Stokes and Easton, 2015, pp. 145, 147.

- The Technical Department (also known as the Third Department), which was responsible for signals intelligence and computer network operations and thus could be expected to be involved in the collection of foreign satellite communications.[94]
- The Electronic Countermeasures and Radar Department (also known as the Fourth Department), which was responsible for EW and radar. Its space-related roles included jamming satellite communications and the GPS signal.[95]
- The Informatization Department, which was responsible for managing the PLA's communications network, including satellite communications.[96]
- The Satellite Navigation Office (中国卫星导航系统管理办), which was an interagency organization that was led by the GSD and was responsible for the development, promotion, and industrialization of China's BeiDou satellite navigation system.[97]

The GSD, the Second Artillery, and the PLAAF also played a role in China's space enterprise. The Second Artillery and the PLAAF both appeared to be involved in missile defense, while the Second Artillery appeared to be responsible for direct-ascent kinetic kill missions and mobile satellite launch.

In addition to the military, civilian organizations also played a role in China's space enterprise. The State Administration for Science, Technology and Industry for National Defense (SASTIND) is a regulatory and policymaking body that governs the work of the defense industry, including the space industry. SASTIND is also in charge of China's lunar exploration program. Subordinate to SASTIND is the China National Space Administration, which oversees the work of the space industry.

China also has a number of organizations responsible for collecting, processing, and disseminating remote sensing information. These include

- The National Remote Sensing Center of China (中国遥感中心), which is subordinate to the Ministry of Science and Technology.
- The Center for Resources Satellite Data and Application (中国资源卫星应用中心), which is subordinate to SASTIND and the National Development and Reform Commission.
- The National Meteorological Satellite Center (国家卫星气象中心), which is subordinate to the China National Meteorological Administration.

---

[94] Stokes and Easton, 2015, p. 148.

[95] Stokes and Easton, 2015, pp. 157-158.

[96] Stokes and Easton, 2015, p. 151.

[97] China Satellite Navigation Office, "Report on the Development of the BeiDou Satellite Navigation System (Version 2.2)," December 2013, p. 1.

- The Satellite Surveying and Mapping Application Center (国家测绘地理信息局卫星测绘应用中心), which is subordinate to the Ministry of Land and Resources' State Bureau of Surveying and Mapping of China.
- The China National Satellite Ocean Application Service (中国卫星海洋应用中心), which is also subordinate to the Ministry of Land and Resources' State Oceanic Administration.

The CAS also operates a number of space-related organizations involved in space science and earth remote sensing. These include astronomical observatories and a number of research institutes, such as the Shanghai Institute of Optics and Fine Mechanics (lasers), the Institute of Optics, Fine Mechanics, and Physics (optics), and the Institute of High Energy Physics (lasers). Although the mission of the CAS is primarily science-related, the dual-use nature of space technologies indicates that the CAS may play a role in military operations. For example, its role in astronomical observation may be useful in providing space situational awareness. The Shanghai Astronomical Observatory employs laser range-finders that can determine the range of an object in space to within 50–70 centimeters.[98] Its work on lasers may also hold the possibility of the CAS playing a counterspace role. In addition, the CAS operates three remote sensing data stations—in Beijing, Sanya, and Kashgar—that can receive remote sensing data from satellites.

China's Post-Reform Space Enterprise

China's pre-reform space enterprise was characterized by numerous entities organized into GSD, GAD, service, and civilian stovepipes, with no one agency overseeing all of the military's space operations. China's post-reform space enterprise retains this feature, with the functions of the GSD and GAD, such as satellite launch and operations, being transferred to the SSF. There is no evidence that this reform transferred other important aspects of China's space program to the SSF, however.

We found no evidence that units subordinated to the services have been handed over to the SSF or that units responsible for direct-ascent counterspace missions, missile defense, and mobile satellite launch have been subordinated to the SSF.[99] In fact, the PLAAF maintains that it continues to carry out its "integrated air and space warfare" mission through its missile defense units. On August 28, 2016, the day before President Xi conducted his first visit to the SSF, an article appearing in the official Chinese press on the PLAAF's air and missile defense capabilities stated that its "air defense troops conduct innovation-driven development to form an integrated short, medium, long-range and low, medium, and high altitude operational system to

---

[98] "Our Country's Substantial Achievements in Countering the Threat of Space Debris" (我国应对空间碎片威胁成果丰硕), Ministry of Industry and Information Technology, May 19, 2014.

[99] It is important to note, however, that given the secretive nature of many aspects of China's military space program, it seems likely that the PLA would seek to conceal some details of the reorganization.

completely advance an air and missile defense capability under informatized conditions and to build a blue sky shield to defend the country's air and space security."[100]

There is also no evidence indicating that civilian space organizations have been subordinated to the SSF or that units involved in the GAD's R&D apparatus have been transferred to the SSF. The operational nature of the SSF and the creation of an Equipment Development Department (EDD) under the CMC may have obviated the need for the SSF to inherit these organizations. Nevertheless, the SSF is involved in R&D programs as the operator of China's satellite launch and control centers. SSF deputy commander Major General Liu Shangfu, for example, has also been identified as a deputy commander of China's lunar exploration program.[101] Oddly, however, based on evidence cited previously, at least one GSD research institute appears to have been subordinated to the SSF rather than the EDD.

The SSF also does not command the China Manned Space Agency (CMSA). Formerly under the GAD, the CMSA has been placed under the EDD.[102] Four possible reasons may account for this. First, it may be that the human spaceflight program is still considered a development program and will not be completely operational until China completes a 60-ton space station by 2023. Second, placing the CMSA within an operational military organization may connote an overt militarization of China's human spaceflight program that could serve as an obstacle to cooperation with potential foreign partners such as the National Aeronautics and Space Administration (NASA) or the European Space Agency and call into question China's stated commitment to the peaceful use of outer space. A third possible reason is that the PLA may consider the manned spaceflight program of minimal value to military operations. This possibility, it should be noted, would be at odds with assessments by many Chinese analysts who regard manned military missions as more capable than robotic missions.[103] The fourth, and perhaps most logical, reason involves the nature of the human spaceflight program as a national-level R&D program. The program requires a commander of sufficient rank who can command the more than 3,000 organizations from across the military and various government ministries that have been involved in the endeavor. This role has fallen to the director of the GAD, whose military rank placed him above even government ministers and gave him a direct line to the president of China. Although the new EDD formed under the CMC plays a diminished role in

---

[100] "China's Air Force Advances the Building of Air and Missile Defenses to Form an Integrated Short, Medium, Long Range and Low, Medium, and High Altitude Operational System" (中国空军加快推进防空反导能力建设 形成远中近程高中低空相结合的作战体系), *Xinhua*, August 28, 2016.

[101] "The Third Stage of the Lunar Exploration Project Chang'e 5 Transitions to the Final Research and Development Stage," 2016.

[102] "CASC Convenes 2016 Work Meeting" (航天科技集团召开 2016 年度工作会议), China Aerospace Science and Technology Corporation, 2016.

[103] See, for example, Li Yiyong, Li Zhi, and Shen Huairong, "Analysis on Development and Application of Near Space Vehicle" (临近空间飞行器发展与应用分析), *Journal of the Academy of Equipment Command and Technology* (装备指挥技术学院学报), 2008/2, p. 64; and Chang Xianqi, *Military Astronautics* (军事航天学), pp. 118–119.

the PLA bureaucracy, by retaining former GAD head Zhang Youxia as its commander, it remains capable of providing comprehensive leadership of the entire human spaceflight program.

As a result, the evidence to date supports only the SSF carrying out the launch and management of China's space-based C4ISR assets. The only counterspace role for the SSF in this context supported by sources is the co-orbital mission using weaponized satellites to attack other satellites. Other counterspace-related missions appear to reside within the SSF, but not within its space systems unit. The network systems unit, for example, could be responsible for the EW mission against satellite communications and navigation signals and the cyber mission against ground-based space facilities and satellites.

Nevertheless, this does not mean that counterspace elements from the Rocket Force or the Air Force have not been transferred to the SSF. The Chinese military has been very tight-lipped about its counterspace efforts and, with the exception of its 2007 ASAT test, has never acknowledged the existence of ASAT development programs. Thus, the PLA may never openly acknowledge the existence of a counterspace role for any unit, including the SSF, or it may provide only very general and limited information on this part of its mission.

6. Conclusions

The PLA's reform effort, which was initiated on December 31, 2015, is intended to enable the PLA to fight and win modern wars against a highly technologically advanced adversary. A major part of this effort has been organizational reform designed to enable the PLA to conduct joint operations. A major part of the organizational reform has been the establishment of the SSF, a new organization designed to better integrate space, cyber, and EW capabilities into PLA operations. Although scant official information exists on the SSF, the available evidence indicates that the SSF appears to be composed of former GSD and GAD units.

In carrying out its role, the SSF does not appear to be a service, nor does it appear to be a U.S. military-style unified command. Although a small number of Air Force and Navy personnel serve in the SSF, their role remains unclear, and it could be that they serve a liaison function rather than an operational role. Therefore, the SSF does appear to be a unique organization—one primarily staffed by Army personnel but tasked with the inherently joint mission of supporting all services with its space, cyber, and EW capabilities. The SSF is thus at the forefront of the PLA's drive to develop joint capabilities to fight "informatized local wars."

The importance of the SSF's space role is reflected in official and unofficial sources on the SSF's leadership and units. The appointment of LTG Gao Jin as the commander of the SSF may be instructive, for two reasons. His experience as a Second Artillery officer provided him with operational experience in a space-related field. Perhaps more importantly, his position as the commandant of the AMS placed him at the front lines of the PLA's efforts to understand and adapt to fighting informatized wars, a background that might prove essential as the SSF becomes more established and its role is better defined. The official identification of Major General Liu Shangfu as a deputy commander of the SSF and a former commander of the Xichang Satellite Launch Center is also a strong indicator of the SSF's role in China's space program. Identification of former GAD officers involved in China's space program also supports the assessment that the SSF runs the military's space program.

The SSF fulfills its space mission role in two ways. The first and main function of the SSF in regard to space is C4ISR support to an operational force through its computer network, communications, and space-operations functions. The SSF's C4ISR capabilities provide the connective tissue between units that enables the PLA to effectively conduct joint operations and successfully prosecute "system vs. system warfare" that the PLA characterizes as essential to winning modern wars. The SSF fulfills this role by launching and operating China's satellite architecture, although its role in providing mobile space launch capabilities remains unclear. With its capabilities, the SSF plays a critical role in supporting the types of aerospace power projection operations the PLA expects it will need to conduct in future scenarios.

President Xi's urging to use civil-military integration (军民融合) to carry out the SSF's mission suggests that the force will also integrate civilian entities into its operations. According to the 2015 defense white paper, civil-military integration involves "joint building and utilization of military and civilian infrastructure, joint exploration of the sea, outer space and air, and shared use of such resources as surveying and mapping, navigation, meteorology and frequency spectra" to make "military and civilian resources … more compatible, complementary and mutually accessible." Integrating civilian organizations into military operations appears to play an important role in China's space and cyber operations. Many civilian organizations, including the Ministry of Science and Technology, the Chinese Meteorological Administration, and the CAS, play a role in China's space program and would appear to be an essential component if space operations are to be conducted effectively.

Another important space function is the counterspace mission. Although information on this issue remains incomplete, the SSF's Space Systems Department appears to be charged with carrying out the co-orbital counterspace mission involving satellite-on-satellite attacks. It could logically be expected to take on responsibility for other counterspace missions as well, although Chinese publications provide little information on direct-ascent ASAT and directed-energy weapons capabilities due to the secretive nature of China's counterspace program.

Other counterspace functions performed by the SSF appear to be carried out by its Network Systems Department, which appears to be responsible for jamming satellite communications and GPS signals, as well as hacking into the computer systems of space facilities and their satellites. The main direct warfighting role of the SSF overall appears to be in the cyber and electromagnetic domains (a role that is beyond the scope of this report). As a result, the SSF appears to be an organizational response to the PLA concept of integrated-network EW that emphasizes combining cyber and EW forces into a joint force.[104] Additionally, because PLA strategists view space and cyber warfare as important components of strategic deterrence alongside nuclear and conventional forces, the SSF would also appear to be poised to play an important role in China's further development of its strategic deterrence posture and in the conduct of deterrence operations.

The exact process of SSF support to PLA joint operations remains to be seen. Although it is reasonable to assume that SSF units will be attached to a theater command during military operations, whether the SSF will augment forces below the theater command level is unknown. For example, the Chinese publications we examined do not address the position of technical reconnaissance bureaus that were formerly assigned to the MRs but were part of a system overseen by the former GSD Third Department. Based on recent analysis, however, there appears to be some bifurcation of duties between the SSF and the CMC Joint Staff Department's

---

[104] See, for example, Kevin Pollpeter, "Controlling the Information Domain: Space, Cyber, and Electronic Warfare," in Ashley Tellis and Travis Tanner, eds., *Strategic Asia: 2012-13: China's Military Challenge*, Seattle, Wash.: National Bureau of Asian Research, 2012, pp. 181–182.

Information and Communications Bureau, with the SSF responsible for *information support*— i.e., pursuing intelligence, surveillance, and reconnaissance to enable operational and strategic objectives during joint operations—and the Information and Communications Bureau responsible for *information assurance*—i.e., ensuring the integrity and functionality of command and control information and communications systems.[105] In reality, the two will most likely need to engage in some degree of coordination and information-sharing during joint operations.

Some of these unknowns will probably become clearer as the PLA conducts major military exercises that incorporate the SSF, highlighting how its capabilities will support other PLA forces. For example, official media reports recently stated that the SSF, PLAAF, and Ground Forces from all five theater commands participated in a major military exercise from July to September 2016 at the Zhurihe training base in Inner Mongolia.[106] As details from such exercises become available, this will likely illuminate the process by which the SSF supports other components of the PLA.

Another important unknown is how the SSF's Space Systems Department coordinates with the military services and civilian agencies that also perform space missions. It would appear that some sort of joint command under the theater command would need to be established to lead an operation's space forces. For example, if the Rocket Force is responsible for direct-ascent ASAT missions, SSF units providing space situational awareness would need some sort of mechanism to inform Rocket Force units of the orbital position of targeted satellites. PLA consumers of space-based C4ISR would also need a command-and-control structure to request space products, such as satellite imagery.

The lack of a clear command-and-control structure to govern all aspects of the PLA's space enterprise brings up the question of whether the PLA will establish a space force. China's post-reform space enterprise appears to do little to ameliorate the fragmented nature of the space program. In fact, the PLA could have enacted a more drastic set of organizational reforms, such as establishing an executive agent for space, as urged by some commentators, or giving the entire space mission to a particular service, as some PLAAF and Second Artillery analysts argued would be necessary to ensure the most effective use of military space capabilities. Such a move would require wrenching space-related forces from the services and giving them to the SSF or a newly created independent "Space Force." As stated earlier, it appears that the PLA has judged this move premature, and it could be contingent upon space becoming an independent campaign.

Based on these assessments, the main purpose of establishing the SSF appears to be twofold: First, it made one organization responsible for the development of the PLA's space and information-warfare forces to better integrate their capabilities into a joint force. The PLA's view of the essential nature of space and information operations to modern warfighting suggests that

---

[105] Elsa Kania, "PLA Strategic Support Force: The 'Information Umbrella' for China's Military," *The Diplomat*, April 1, 2017.

[106] Yao Jianing, "Chinese Army to Kick Off Three Month Drill," *Xinhua*, July 14, 2016.

the military decided to entrust these crucial missions to one dedicated organization that would not be burdened with the legacy missions of the services or the R&D focus of the former GAD. Ultimately, however, the purpose of the SSF is to serve the PLA's overall reform effort by making the PLA into a joint force capable of effectively responding to contingencies. It is not necessarily intended to completely rationalize the organizational structure of China's broader space enterprise.

A second and more practical purpose may be bureaucratic. The downgrading of the four general departments necessitated the need for indispensable units under the GSD and GAD to be placed under some other command. Rather than determining which services would inherit which units, a bureaucratically easier option appears to have been to create a separate organization that could absorb these units. This could have been seen as a means of avoiding a sharp competition between the PLAAF and the Rocket Force over the relevant resources and capabilities. Similarly, the reduction of the seven MRs to five theater commands not only necessitated the elimination of units but also made personnel redundant. The creation of the SSF, along with the assigning of personnel from the MRs to staff it, suggests that the PLA has used the SSF to retain officers that were passed over for MR billets. Although the pedigrees of many of the SSF's leadership indicate that they are qualified for their positions, they also reflect that some in the leadership, especially the political commissars, have no indicated prior experience in space, cyber, or EW. As time passes and as younger officers rise through the ranks, this can be expected to change.

At this point in the PLA's restructuring, it is not surprising that many questions remain. The SSF is a work in progress. The PLA expects the implementation of the latest reforms to take several more years, concluding in 2020. The announcement of the SSF's establishment, along with the news of other aspects of the PLA reorganization on December 31, 2015, suggests that the deadline for its founding may have been based on a predetermined date, such as the end of the 12th Five-Year Plan, rather than on the actual readiness of the PLA to fully implement the envisioned reforms. A statement by SSF PC Liu Fulian that many "contradictions"[107] need to be resolved and news articles encouraging SSF personnel to begin in-depth study of the nature and mission of the SSF and to practice "military democracy" in this exploration also suggest that the PLA is still figuring out exactly how the SSF will carry out its mission.[108] The assessment in another article that the development of a "construction plan" for the SSF is a severe test for the PLA suggests both that planning for the makeup of the force is incomplete and that it will be difficult.[109]

---

[107] Li Guoli and Sun Yanxin, "Representative Liu Fulian: High Standards and High Goals Will Build a Strong and Modern Strategic Support Force" (刘福连代表：高标准高起点建设强大的现代化战略支援部队), *China Military Online* (中国军网), March 9, 2016.

[108] Zong Zhaodun, "The Strategic Support Force, Redefining War and Peace" (战略支援部队，重新定义战争与和平), *Liberation Reporter* (解放记者), January 15, 2016.

[109] Zong Zhaodun and Zou Weirong, "Strategic Support Force Builds and Develops New Type Operational Forces" (战略支援部队建设发展新型作战力量), *Liberation Reporter* (解放记者), January 27, 2016.

The significance of the SSF's establishment should not be underestimated, however. The pathway provided by the SSF to further develop the PLA's information-warfare forces, including its space forces, opens the door for these capabilities to be further integrated into PLA warfighting through the development of both doctrine and personnel. The establishment of an organization charged with the information-warfare mission suggests that principles need to be established to guide its wartime use and peacetime development. The creation of the SSF would also seem to suggest that avenues for the promotion of information warfighters and their integration into theater command operations will need to be developed. In summary, information warfare, including space warfare, long identified by PLA analysts as a critical element of warfare, appears to have entered a period of significant development that could critically affect U.S. military operations. Indeed, Chinese military strategists see military space operations as a key component of strategic deterrence, as a critical means of countering U.S. military intervention in the region, and as increasingly important to supporting operations aimed at protecting China's emerging interests in more-distant locations.

References

Academic Divisions of the Chinese Academy of Sciences, homepage, undated. As of July 18, 2017:
  http://www.casad.cas.cn/aca/371/xxjskxb-201512-t20151224_4502666.html

"Adhere to Innovation Driven Development Promote Military Innovation Capabilities" (坚持创新驱动发展 提升军事创新能力), Ministry of National Defense website, April 4, 2016. As of July 18, 2017:
  http://www.mod.gov.cn/topnews/2016-04/09/content_4648861.htm

All-Army Military Terminology Management Committee, *Chinese People's Liberation Army Military Terminology* (中国人民解放军军语), Beijing: Military Science Press, 2011, p. 332.

An Puzhong, Ouyang Hao, and Du Kang, "Keeping a Clean Political Environment – Military NPC Representatives Eager Building Work Style" (永葆绿水青山的政治生态—军队人大代表热议作风建设), *China Military Online* (中国军网), March 10, 2016. As of July 18, 2017:
  http://www.81.cn/2016qglh/2016-03/10/content_6952935.htm

"Announcement of Tender for New Space Electronic Equipment," (航天装备新品电子元器件科研项目招标公告), All Military Weapons and Equipment Purchasing Information Network (全军武器装备采购信息网), August 4, 2016. As of July 18, 2017:
  http://www.weain.mil.cn/cggg/zbgg/527557.html

Barbosa, Rui C., "China launches Jilin-1 mission via Long March 2D," NASASpaceFlight.com, October 7, 2015. As of July 18, 2017:
  http://www.nasaspaceflight.com/2015/10/china-launches-jilin-1-mission-long-march-2d/

———, "China's Shenzhou 9 Successfully Docks with Tiangong-1," NASASpaceFlight.com, June 18, 2012. As of July 18, 2017:
  https://www.nasaspaceflight.com/2012/06/chinas-shenzhou-9-successfully-docks-with-tiangong-1/

"Beijing MR Political Commissar Liu Fulian Biography" (北京军区政委刘福连简历" Ta Kong Pao, July 31, 2013. As of July 23, 2017:
  http://news.takungpao.com/mainland/focus/2013-07/1798971.html

"CASC Convenes 2016 Work Meeting" (航天科技集团召开 2016 年度工作会议), China Aerospace Science and Technology Corporation, 2016. As of July 18, 2017:
  http://www.spacechina.com/n25/n144/n206/n214/c1158291/content.html

37

Chandrashekar, S., and Soma Perumal, *China's Constellation of Yaogan Satellites & the Anti-Ship Ballistic Missile: May 2016 Update*, Bangalore, India: National Institute of Advanced Studies, May 2016. As of July 18, 2017:
http://isssp.in/wp-content/uploads/2016/05/Yaogan-and-ASBM May-2016-Report.pdf

Chang Xianqi, *Military Astronautics* (军事航天学), Beijing: National Defense Industry Press, 2002.

"China Announces Success in Technology to Refuel Satellites in Orbit," *Xinhua*, June 30, 2016. As of July 18, 2017:
http://news.xinhuanet.com/english/2016-06/30/c_135479061.htm

"China PLA GSD 58th Research Institute" (中国人民解放军总参第五十八研究所), China Graduate Student Enrollment Information Network, September 13, 2016. As of July 23, 2017:
http://yz.chsi.com.cn/sch/schoolInfo--schId-367828.dhtml

"China PLA Strategic Support Force Network Systems Department 56th Research Institute" (中国人民解放军战略支援部队网络系统部第五十六研究所), China Graduate Student Enrollment Information Network, May 27, 2017. As of July 23, 2017:
http://yz.chsi.com.cn/sch/schoolInfo--schId-368175.dhtml

"China's Air Force Advances the Building of Air and Missile Defenses Forms an Integrated Short, Medium, Long Range and Low, Medium, and High Altitude Operational System" (中国空军加快推进防空反导能力建设 形成远中近程高中低空相结合的作战体系), *Xinhua*, August 28, 2016. As of July 18, 2017:
http://news.xinhuanet.com/politics/2016-08/28/c_1119467422.htm

China Satellite Navigation Office, "Report on the Development of the BeiDou Satellite Navigation System (Version 2.2)," December 2013.

China's Military Strategy, State Council Information Office of the People's Republic of China, Ministry of Defense, May 2015.

"China's New Orbital Debris Clean-Up Satellite Raises Space Militarization Concerns," Spaceflight101.com, June 29, 2016. As of July 18, 2017:
http://spaceflight101.com/long-march-7-maiden-launch/aolong-1-asat-concerns/

"China's Ocean Satellites" (中国海洋卫星), *Aerospace China* (中国航天), No. 372, April 2009.

"Class-A Qualification List for Integrated Information System" (涉密信息系统集成甲级资质单位名录), National Secrecy Science and Technology Evaluation Center (国家保密科技测评中心), November 18, 2016.

Costello, John, "China Finally Centralizes Its Space, Cyber, Information Forces," *The Diplomat*, January 20, 2016. As of July 18, 2017:
http://thediplomat.com/2016/01/china-finally-its-centralizes-space-cyber-information-forces/

"Decision of the Central Committee of the Communist Party of China on Some Major Issues Concerning Comprehensively Deepening the Reform," *Xinhua*, January 16, 2014. As of July 18, 2017:
http://www.china.org.cn/china/third_plenary_session/2014-01/16/content_31212602_15.htm

"Expert Says the Strategic Support Force Independently Becomes a Military Concept Ahead of the U.S. Military" (专家称战略支援部队独立成军 理念领先于美军) ,sina.com, January 8, 2016. As of July 18, 2017:
http://mil.news.sina.com.cn/china/2016-01-08/doc-ifxnkkuy7732953.shtml

"Expert: The Strategic Support Force Will Be Critical for Victory During the Entire Operation" (专家:战略支援部队将贯穿作战全过程 是致胜关键), *People's Daily Online* (人民网), January 5, 2016. As of July 18, 2017:
http://military.people.com.cn/n1/2016/0105/c1011-28011251.html

Finkelstein, David, "2015 Should be an Exciting Year for PLA-Watching," *Pathfinder Magazine*, Vol. 13, No. 1, Winter 2015.

Flaherty, Mary Pat, Jason Samenow, and Lisa Rein, "Chinese Hack U.S. Weather Systems, Satellite Network," *Washington Post*, November 12, 2014.

"Full Text of Hu Jintao's Report at 18th Party Congress," *Xinhua*, November 17, 2012. As of July 18, 2017:
http://news.xinhuanet.com/english/special/18cpcnc/2012-11/17/c_131981259_10.htm

"Gao Jin Becomes PLA's Youngest Military Region-Level Chief," *Want China Times*, December 25, 2014. As of July 23, 2017:
https://web.archive.org/web/20150702025656/http://www.wantchinatimes.com/news-subclass-cnt.aspx?id=20141225000091&cid=1601

"General Staff Personnel Changes Wang Huiqing Becomes Strategic Planning Department Director Zheng Junie Becomes Third Department Director" (总参人事变动王辉青任战略规划部部长郑俊杰任三部), 163.com, November 1, 2015.

Grossman, Elaine M., "Top Commander: Chinese Interference with U.S. Satellites Uncertain," *World Politics Review,* October 18, 2006.

Guo Yuandan, "Want to Fight Naval Wars? China Should Prepare for Naval Combat" (要打海上战争？中国应做海上军事斗争准备), mil.huanqiu.com. As of July 18, 2017:
http://mil.huanqiu.com/strategysituation/2015-05/6526726_2.html

Jiang Lianju and Wang Liwen, eds., *Textbook for the Study of Space Operations* （空间作战靴
教程）, Beijing: Military Science Publishing House, 2013.

Kania, Elsa, "PLA Strategic Support Force: The 'Information Umbrella' for China's Military,"
The Diplomat, April 1, 2017.

"Laser Ranging Systems Project Sole Source Announcement" (激光探测定位系统项目单一来源采购
公示公告), Beijing Guotai Jianzhong Management and Consulting Co. Ltd., October 31, 2016.
As of July 23, 2017:
http://www.bjgtjz.com/newsview.asp?nid=11478

Li Guoli and Sun Yanxin, "Representative Liu Fulian: High Standards and High Goals Will
Build a Strong and Modern Strategic Support Force (刘福连代表：高标准高起点建设强大
的现代化战略支援部队), *China Military Online* (中国军网), March 9, 2016. As of July 18,
2017:
http://www.81.cn/jmywyl/2016-03/09/content_6952963.htm

Li Yiyong, Li Zhi, and Shen Huairong, "Analysis on Development and Application of Near
Space Vehicle" (临近空间飞行器发展与应用分析)," *Journal of the Academy of Equipment
Command and Technology* (装备指挥技术学院学报), 2008/2, p. 64.

"Liberation Army Daily: Form Unique Advantages in R&D Competition" (解放军报：在科研
必争领域形成独特优势）, CCP Information Network (中国共产党信息网), March 22,
2016. As of July 18, 2017:
http://theory.people.com.cn/n1/2016/0322/c49150-28216331.html

"Liu Fulian Becomes Deputy Commander and Chief of Staff of the Strategic Support Force" (李
尚福任战略支援部队副司令员兼参谋长(图)), Huanqiu.com, February 9, 2016. As of
July 18, 2017:
http://china.huanqiu.com/article/2016-02/8627072.html

"Long March 3B Lofts Gaofen-4 to Close Out 2015," NASASpaceFlight.com, December 28,
2015. As of July 18, 2017:
http://www.nasaspaceflight.com/2015/12/long-march-3b-gaofen-4-close-2015/

"Major General Feng Jianhua Will Transfer to be Strategic Support Force Political Department
Director" (冯建华少将调任战略支援部队政治部主任), news.sohu.com, February 28, 2016.
As of July 18, 2017:
http://news.sohu.com/20160228/n438780064.shtml

Martin, Paul K., Inspector General, National Aeronautics and Space Administration, "NASA
Cyber Security: An Examination of the Agency's Information Security," Testimony Before
the Subcommittee on Investigations and Oversight, House Committee on Science, Space, and

Technology, February 29, 2012. As of August 6, 2017:
https://oig.nasa.gov/congressional/FINAL_written_statement_for_%20IT_%20hearing_February_26_cdit_v2.pdf

McCauley, Kevin, "System of System Operational Capability: Key Supporting Concepts for Future Joint Operations," *China Brief*, October 5, 2012. As of July 18, 2017:
http://www.jamestown.org/single/?no_cache=1&tx_ttnews%5Btt_news%5D=39932#.Venjn WeFOh1

"Members of the Strategic Support Force Leadership Group Includes Space Force and Cyber Force Commanders and PCs Generals for the Four General Departments Take Positions" (战略支援部队首任领导班子成员 包括天军网军司令政委 四总部将领履新), blog.sina.cn, January 8, 2016. As of July 18, 2017:
http://blog.sina.cn/dpool/blog/s/blog_4a7db6a70102w4dy.html?vt=4

Mu Zhiyong, "Paying Attention to the Construction of Integrated Information and Information System," *Study Times*, September 17, 2015. As of July 18, 2017:
http://www.ccps.gov.cn/xxsb/xxsb_20150917/201509/t20150917_66349.html

Ni Guanghui, "Our Military's Secretive First Strategic Support Force" (揭秘我军首支战略支援部队), *China Military Online* (中国军网), January 24, 2016. As of July 18, 2017:
http://www.81.cn/jwzl/2016-01-24/content_6866922.htm

"Nie Rongzhen Feared Corrupt S&T Cadres: Early On Checked Them Individually" （聂荣臻怕科技干部冻坏手：早上出操挨个查看), Ecns (中国新闻网), *PLA Daily*, January 28, 2015. As of July 18, 2017:
http://www.chinanews.com/mil/2015/01-28/7010910.shtml

Office of the Secretary of Defense, *Annual Report to Congress: Military and Security Developments Involving the People's Republic of China 2011*, U.S. Department of Defense, 2011.

———, *Annual Report to Congress: Military and Security Developments Involving the People's Republic of China 2015*, U.S. Department of Defense, 2015.

"Our Country's Substantial Achievements in Countering the Threat of Space Debris" (我国应对空间碎片威胁成果丰硕), Ministry of Industry and Information Technology of the People's Republic of China, May 19, 2014.

"Partial List of Expert Report Topics," *Journal of Radars*, Excel spreadsheet, undated. As of July 23, 2017:
http://radars.ie.ac.cn/UserFiles/File/2016%E9%95%BF%E6%98%A5%E9%9B%B7%E8%BE%BE%E4%B8%8E%E5%AF%B9%E6%8A%97%E7%A0%94%E8%AE%A8%E4%BC%9A%E6%8A%A5%E5%91%8A-1025.pdf

PLA Academy of Military Science (AMS) Military Strategy Studies Department, *Science of Military Strategy* (战略学), Beijing: Military Science Press, December 2013.

Pollpeter, Kevin, "China's Space Doctrine," in Andrew S. Erickson and Lyle J. Goldstein, eds., *Chinese Aerospace Power*, Annapolis, Md.: Naval Institute Press, 2011.

———, "China's Space Robotic Arm Programs," *SITC News Analysis*, October 2013. As of July 23, 2017:
http://escholarship.org/uc/item/2js0c5r8

———, "Controlling the Information Domain: Space, Cyber, and Electronic Warfare," in Ashley Tellis and Travis Tanner, eds., *Strategic Asia: 2012–13: China's Military Challenge*, Seattle, Wash.: National Bureau of Asian Research, 2012.

———, "The PLAAF and the Integration of Air and Space Power," in Richard P. Hallion, Roger Cliff, and Phillip C. Saunders, eds., *The Chinese Air Force: Evolving Concepts, Roles, and Capabilities*, Washington, D.C.: National Defense University Press, 2012.

Pollpeter, Kevin, Eric Anderson, and Fan Yang, *China Dream, Space Dream: China's Progress in Space Technologies and Implications for the United States*, Institute on Global Conflict and Cooperation, March 2015.

Qin Lixin and Zhang Yi, "A Limited Definition of System Integration" (体系融合小意), Ministry of National Defense website, November 12, 2015. As of July 18, 2017:
http://www.mod.gov.cn/intl/2015-11/12/content_4628404.htm

Qiu Yue, "Our Military's Strategic Support Force Is What Type of Military Force?" (我军战略支援部队是一支什么样的军事力量？), *China Military Online* (中国军网), January 5, 2016. As of July 18, 2017:
http://www.81.cn/jwgz/2016-01/05/content_6844493.htm

Ren Xu, "Ministry of National Defense Spokesperson Takes Media Inquiries on Deepening National Defense and Military Reform" (国防部新闻发言人就深化国防和军队改革有关问题接受媒体专访), *China Military Net* (中国军网), January 1, 2016. As of July 18, 2017:
http://www.81.cn/jmywyl/2016-01/01/content_6839936.htm

"Rocket Force, Strategic Support Force Support Joint Readiness During the Spring Festival" (火箭军、战略支援部队等军种春节联合战备), *Liberation Reporter* (解放记者), February 10, 2016. As of July 18, 2017:
http://zb.81.cn/content/2016-02/10/content_6903319.htm

"Scientists: China Should Integrate Space Resources to Improve Emergency Response," *People's Daily Online*, March 4, 2009. As of July 18, 2017:
http://english.people.com.cn/90001/90781/90876/6605410.html

Stokes, Mark, and Ian Easton, "The Chinese People's Liberation Army General Staff Department: Evolving Organization and Missions," in Kevin Pollpeter and Kenneth W. Allen, eds., *PLA as Organization V2.0*, Vienna, Va.: Defense Group, Inc., 2015.

"The CMC's Opinions on Deepening National Defense and Military Reform" (中央军委关于深化国防和军队改革的意见 (全文)), January 1, 2016. As of July 18, 2017: http://www.81.cn/jmywyl/2016-01/01/content_6839904.htm

"The Reader for Chairman Xi Jinping's Important Expositions on National Defense and Military Reform (2016 Edition) on Resolutely Winning the Battle to Deepen National Defense and Military Reform—On Completely Implementing the Strategy on Reforming and Strengthening the Military" (习主席国防和军队建设重要论述读本（2016 年版）坚决打赢深化国防和军队改革这场攻坚战—关于全面实施改革强军战略), *Liberation Army Daily* (解放军报), May 26, 2016.

"The Scoop: Two Major Generals Become Commanders of the Strategic Support Force" (独家报道：两少将任战略支援部队副司令) ,*Da Gong Bao* (大公报), January 6, 2016. As of July 18, 2017. http://news.takungpao.com/mainland/focus/2016-01/3264096.html

"The Strategic Support Force is Actually a Space-Cyber Force: It Will Change Warfare"(战略支援部队其实就是天网军：将改变战争), war.163.com, November 1, 2015. As of July 18, 2017: http://war.163.com/16/0104/08/BCFMF4HF00014J0G.html

"The Third Stage of the Lunar Exploration Project Chang'e 5 Transitions to the Final Research and Development Stage" (探月三期嫦娥五号任务转入正样研制阶段), State Administration for Science and Technology and Industry for National Defense, February 19, 2016. As of July 18, 2017: http://www.sastind.gov.cn/n112/n117/c6329847/content.html

Union of Concerned Scientists, *UCS Satellite Database: In-Depth Details on the 1,459 Satellites Currently Orbiting Earth*, undated, last revised April 11, 2017. As of July 18, 2017: http://www.ucsusa.org/nuclear-weapons/space-weapons/satellite-database#.VvVXc2b2YqQ

Wang Jun, "Chengdu MR Political Department Director Liang Chaishao Changes Positions to Become MR Deputy PC" (成都军区政治部主任柴绍良改任军区副政委), *Dagong Bao* (大公报), December 31, 2013. As of July 18, 2017: http://news.takungpao.com/mainland/zgzq/2013-12/2143144.html

"Wang Jun Meets Wang Zhaoyu, Liu Jianguo, and Han Qiang" (王君会见王兆宇刘建国韩强), CCP Information Network ((中国共产党信息网), February 21, 2013. As of July 18, 2017: http://cpc.people.com.cn/n/2013/0221/c117005-20555625.html

Wang Qiao, Wu Chuanqing, and Li Qing, "Environment Satellite 1 and Its Application in Environmental Monitoring," *Journal of Remote Sensing*, Vol. 1, 2010, p. 104

Wang Shibin and An Puzhong, "Xi Jinping Confers Military Flags to Chinese People's Liberation Army Ground Force, Rocket Force, and Strategic Rocket Force" (习近平向中国人民解放军陆军火箭军战略支援部队授予军旗并致训词), *China Military Net* (中国军网), January 1, 2016. As of July 18, 2017: http://www.81.cn/sydbt/2016-01/01/content_6839896.htm

Wang Shibin, Yin Hang, and Song Xin, "The Best Is to Have a Motivated Heart: Sidelights of President Xi Jinping Meeting with Parts of the Grassroots NPC Representatives (最是深情励军心 -习近平主席接见部分军队基层人大代表侧记), *Liberation Reporter* (解放记者), March 12, 2014. As of July 18, 2017: http://jz.81.cn/n2014/tp/content_5853452.htm

Weeden, Brian, "Dancing in the Dark: The Orbital Rendezvous of SJ-12 and SJ-06F," *Space Review*, August 30, 2010. As of July 18, 2017: http://www.thespacereview.com/article/1689/1

"Xi Jinping Visits Strategic Support Force Organization Today," (习近平今日视察战略支援部队机关), *China News Online* (中国新闻网), August 29, 2016. As of July 18, 2017: http://www.chinanews.com/m/gn/2016/08-29/7987523.shtml

Yang Yunfang, "The Strategic Support Force Joint Victory" (战略支援部队新型战力联合制胜), *PLA Pictorial* (解放军报), No. 935, 2016.

Yao Jianing, "Chinese Army to Kick Off Three Month Drill," *Xinhua*, July 14, 2016. As of July 18, 2017: http://english.chinamil.com.cn/news-channels/china-military-news/2016-07/14/content_7155592.htm

Yu Jixun (ed.), *Science of Second Artillery Campaigns* (第二炮兵战役学), Beijing: National Defense University Press, 2004.

Zhao Hui, "Problems of Joint Training Under the Information-Technology-Based Condition" (信息化条件下联合训练问题探析), *National Defense Science and Technology* (国防科技工业), Vol. 34, No. 1, February 2013, p. 79.

Zong Zhaodun, "The Strategic Support Force, Redefining War and Peace" (战略支援部队，重新定义战争与和平), *Liberation Reporter* (解放记者), January 15, 2016. As of July 18, 2017:
http://zb.81.cn/content/2016-01/15/content_6882344.htm

Zong Zhaodun and Zou Weirong, "Strategic Support Force Builds and Develops New Type Operational Forces (战略支援部队建设发展新型作战力量), *Liberation Reporter* (解放记者), January 27, 2016. As of July 18, 2017:
http://jz.chinamil.com.cn/gd/2016-01/27/content_6870456.htm

Zou Weirong, "Military NPC Representatives View the Pace of a Strong and Rejuvenated Military (军队人大代表眼中的强军兴军步伐), *People's Daily Online* (人民网), March 15, 2016. As of July 18, 2017:
http://military.people.com.cn/n1/2016/0315/c1011-28200779-3.html